The Official
West Ham United
Annual 2009

Written By Gemma Clarke

A Grange Publication

© 2008. Published by Grange Communications Ltd., Edinburgh, under licence from West Ham United Football Club. Printed in the EU.

Photographs supplied by Arfa Griffiths, Avril Husband, Steve Bacon and John Helliar

ISBN 978 1 906211 48 6

£6.99

Contents

Welcome

Hello and a warm welcome to The Official West Ham United Annual. Here we are in the 2008/09 Barclays Premier League season and all at the club hope it's going to be another exciting and successful one.

The campaign began in fitting style with a special tribute to Bobby Moore. The pre-season game against Villarreal marked the 50th anniversary since the club legend's debut and was staged in his honour. To mark the occasion, the No6 shirt he made famous was retired and formally handed over to his widow Stephanie Moore MBE by Matthew Upson. The England defender had the honour of being the last player to wear the shirt before coming out for the second half of the 1-1 draw wearing No15.

Rekindling memories of the club's proud past was a fitting way to start the new season. The previous campaign was not the easiest but the club still managed to finish in the top ten of the Premier League and all concerned are looking to do even better this time around. What came out of last year was the spirit of the squad. Everyone dug in and when players were asked to play out of position, they did it for the good of the club and picked up results.

With the squad fully fit, the club has the competition in all areas to be an even stronger force in the Premier League, which is the best league in the world. It is certainly the most competitive. No game is a foregone conclusion and that's why people all around the world want to watch it and that's why players from all around the world want to play in it.

This season looks as if it's going to be as competitive as ever. As soon as players reported back to pre-season training, clubs decided that they needed to strengthen their squads. It is no doubt that this season will be even more exciting up and down the country and the talent on show will be second to none.

That is certainly the case with the strong squad assembled by West Ham United. There is the spine of England internationals Robert Green, Matthew Upson, Scott Parker, Kieron Dyer and Dean Ashton along with players with proven international pedigree like Lucas Neill, Valon Behrami, Julien Faubert and Craig Bellamy, who are all vastly experienced.

For younger fans, it is great to see the likes of James Tomkins, Mark Noble, Jack Collison and Freddie Sears continuing to make progress. Like the great Bobby Moore, home-grown players are essential to the development of this club and we will always look to bring through young talent from the Academy.

All the players know everyone reading this Annual wants to follow in their footsteps and become a West Ham United player – and you can be. There are no set rules of what you have to do other than dedicate yourself and keep trying to improve.

A t the top of Green Street, just a short walk from the famous market and a stone's throw from the Boleyn Pub, is the world famous Boleyn Ground – home to West Ham United for more than 100 years.

West Ham United began life as the Thames Iron Works FC, playing their matches at the Memorial Ground at Canning Town but they were asked to vacate the premises at the end of the 1903/04 season.

The Board found that they were allowed to build a new ground on a plot of land next to the Green Street House at Upton Park and agreed to rent the field, which had previously been used to grow potatoes.

The move allowed the Hammers to attract bigger crowds as the total capacity was 20,000 and the new home was easier to get to by rail and tram. The team took their bow at the new Boleyn Ground in a 3-0 win over local rivals Millwall on September 1 1904.

But there were difficult times ahead. In August 1944, during World War II, the south-west corner of the stadium was bombed, forcing the team to play all their fixtures away from home until the repairs were completed.

The Boleyn Ground

In 1995 the North Bank was refurbished and renamed the Centenary Stand and in 2001 the West Stand was replaced by a new 15,000 seat stand named the Dr Martens, which now houses the West Ham United Hotel.

In the 1990s the stadium was modified to become an all-seater in accordance with a directive from the Football Association. In 1993 the South Bank was replaced by a new two-tier 9,000-seat stand named after former captain Bobby Moore.

Hammer of the year

West Ham United's number one, Robert Green, became only the fifth goalkeeper in the club's history to win the prestigious Hammer of the Year award, which he picked up at the end of the 2007/08 season with the lion's share of the fans' vote.

Previous goalkeepers to have won it are Lawrie Leslie, Phil Parkes, Shaka Hislop – and the club's current goalkeeping coach and all-round Hammers legend Ludek Miklosko.

"I'm sure I'll never beat anything Ludo will do!" Robert jokes. "Winning Hammer of the Year is a fantastic honour. You look at the players who've won it before and it's wonderful to be put alongside them. This is a fantastic club and one that is steeped in tradition of having great players.

"To actually be part of it is terrific for me and I'm really pleased to have contributed to what was a successful season. It's been a while since West Ham United finished higher than we did last season. It was a positive campaign that I played my part in and I'm pleased with that."

Going into the 2007/08 season after a year at West Ham United and ten years at Norwich, Robert was yet to save a penalty until the Hammers faced Reading at the Madejski Stadium in September.

He went on to save twice more from the penalty spot, against Portsmouth away and at home to Tottenham Hotspur. He also did enough to put Cristiano Ronaldo off his stride and the Manchester United winger missed his penalty, leading to a 2-1 victory for the Hammers.

"I saved three and one was missed. I hadn't saved one until last season so it was about time something came up! It was pleasing to do that. It's just ironic that you come into the Premier League and start saving penalties. It's something that I'll continue to work on as it's an important part of the game because it's as good as a goal.

"Saving Jermain Defoe's penalty was a personal highlight. Portsmouth was a last minute pen as well. It would have been nice to save them to win games but saving not to lose is equally as important."

And for those hoping to step into Robert's boots one day, the England international has plenty of advice for aspiring young goalkeepers.

"For a start, it's miles easier than running about on the pitch!" he says jokingly. "No, as long as you enjoy your football and enjoy playing in goal, then that's the main thing. It's a difficult position to play in, especially when you're a kid. It's probably harder when you're a kid because people don't tend to have the responsibilities on the pitch that they do as adults, but as long as you enjoy playing your football, that's the main thing.

10 Great Saves from 2007/08

Green v Doyle (Reading, penalty) 1 September 2007

Green v Van Persie (Arsenal) 29 September 2007

Green v Leadbitter (Sunderland) 21 October 2007

Green v Kranjcar (Portsmouth) 27 October 2007

Green v Benjani (Portsmouth, penalty) 27 October 2007

Green v Defoe (Tottenham Hotspur, penalty) 25 November 2007

Green v Tugay (Blackburn Rovers) 9 December 2007

Green v Bullard (Fulham) 23 February 2008

Green v Roberts (Blackburn Rovers) 15 March 2008

Green v Anichebe (Everton) 22 March 2008

"Whatever level you reach if you're enjoying it then you're getting what you want out of the game. It really is a wonderful job and I'm grateful for having what I have. It's been down to hard work and wanting to do my best."

HAMMERS NEWS
Player of the Season

August 2007

11 August 2007 - Barclays Premier League
West Ham United   0   Manchester City   2
Bianchi 18   Geovanni 87
Attendance: 34,921

18 August 2007 - Barclays Premier League
Birmingham City   0   West Ham United   1
Noble 70 (pen)
Attendance: 24,961

25 August 2007 - Barclays Premier League
West Ham United   1   Wigan Athletic   1
Scharner 78   Bowyer 81
Attendance: 33,793

28 August 2007 - Carling Cup, second round
Bristol Rovers   1   West Ham United   2
Bellamy 31, 45   Willams 72
Attendance: 10,831

After a busy pre-season schedule which involved games against Southend United, Dagenham & Redbridge, AS Roma and a sweltering week in Austria, West Ham United kicked off the Barclays Premier League season against Sven-Goran Eriksson's Manchester City at the Boleyn Ground on August 11.

Freddie Ljungberg and Craig Bellamy made their competitive debuts in front of the Hammers fans but Eriksson's Blues were the surprise element in the early part of the season with eight summer signings from abroad. Two of their recent acquisitions, Rolando Bianchi and Geovanni, got on the score sheet at the Boleyn. City notched up three wins in their first three games – including a 1-0 victory over rivals Manchester United.

A rainy afternoon at St Andrews followed for the Hammers with Mark Noble scoring the only goal of the game from the penalty spot in the 70th minute. Recent signing Kieron Dyer impressed on the afternoon with his strength, pace and agility.

Alan Curbishley's men played host to Chris Hutchings' Wigan Athletic side the following week. Paul Scharner put the visitors in front to break the deadlock with just over ten minutes left to play but Lee Bowyer equalised three minutes later to claim his first goal – and a point – for the club.

A testing trip to League One side Bristol Rovers was the final fixture in August and it proved to be a night of mixed emotions for the Hammers. Dyer suffered a double break to his leg in an early challenge and was carried from the field on a stretcher. Bellamy scored a brace to put West Ham United into the hat for the third round draw, although Andy Williams' goal for Rovers led to a late flurry of pressure from Paul Trollope's men. It was a vital win, but came at a high price as Dyer's injury forced   him to miss the remainder of the season.

September 2007

01 September 2007 - Barclays Premier League
Reading   0   West Ham United   3
Bellamy 6   Etherington 49, 90
Attendance: 23,533

15 September 2007 - Barclays Premier League
West Ham United   3   Middlesbrough   0
Bowyer 46   Young 51 (OG)   Ashton 62
Attendance: 34,531

23 September 2007 - Barclays Premier League
Newcastle United   3   West Ham United   1
Viduka 2, 41   Ashton 32   N'Zogbia 76
Attendance: 50,104

26 September 2007 - Carling Cup, third round
West Ham United   1   Plymouth Argyle   0
Ashton 90
Attendance: 25,774

29 September 2007 - Barclays Premier League
West Ham United   0   Arsenal   1
Van Persie 13
Attendance: 34,966

A trip to the north–east followed and an early goal from Newcastle United's Mark Viduka stunned the visiting Hammers and a second strike just before half-time cancelled out Ashton's equaliser. Charles N'Zogbia ensured the Magpies claimed a 3-1 victory in the second half.

Three days later Alan Curbishley's men played host to Championship side Plymouth Argyle in the Carling Cup third round and it looked like a certain stalemate until Ashton let fly with a fierce strike in the 90th minute to ensure a fourth round fixture.

The month ended at the Boleyn Ground with a close contest against Arsene Wenger's title-contending Arsenal side. Robin van Persie's solitary strike after 13 minutes was enough to seal the victory for the visitors.

West Ham United took their winning streak from the end of August into early September with a comprehensive victory over Reading at the Madejski Stadium. Craig Bellamy scored his first Premier League goal of the season for the Hammers, who were in sparkling form.

Matthew Etherington scored an excellent brace and Robert Green made the first penalty save of his career to keep a clean sheet.

The following week, West Ham United notched up another three goals – this time in front of the Boleyn Ground faithful against Gareth Southgate's Middlesbrough. Lee Bowyer opened the scoring early in the second half before Luke Young inadvertently doubled the lead with an own goal five minutes later. Dean Ashton rounded off the scoring to make it a second consecutive 3-0 win.

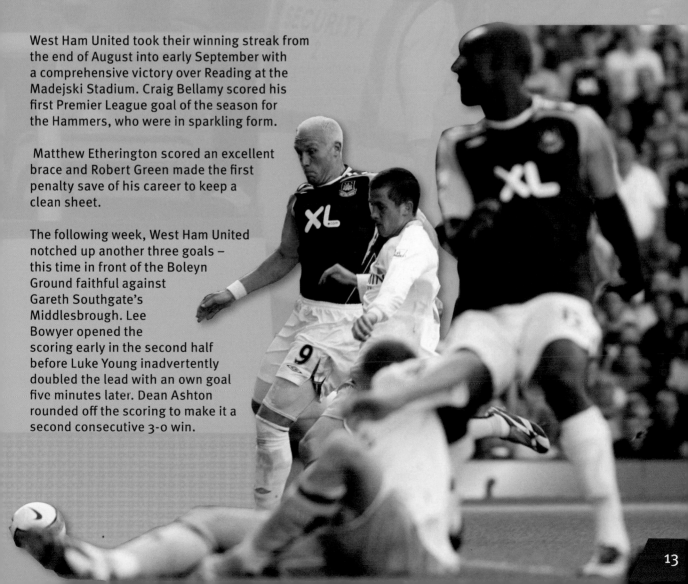

October 2007

06 October 2007 - Barclays Premier League
Aston Villa 1   West Ham United 0
Gardner 24
Attendance: 40,842

21 October 2007 - Barclays Premier League
West Ham United 3   Sunderland 1
Cole 9   Jones 52   Gordon 78 (OG)   Bellamy 90
Attendance: 34,913

27 October 2007 - Barclays Premier League
Portsmouth 0   West Ham United 0
Attendance: 20,525

30 October 2007 - Carling Cup, fourth round
Coventry City 1   West Ham United 2
Tabb 68   Hall 71 (OG)   Cole 90
Attendance: 23,968

October began with a tricky encounter away to Martin O'Neill's high-flying Aston Villa side. Henri Camara put the ball in the net early on for the visitors, but he was judged to have used his hand to deflect Matty Etherington's cross past Scott Carson and promptly booked.

Craig Gardner's fierce free-kick midway through the first half was enough to separate the sides and there was further heartache for the Hammers as Dean Ashton, who had just been called into Steve McLaren's England squad, left the field with a knee ligament injury which ruled him out of international duty.

West Ham United were back to winning ways in their next encounter – a home match against Sunderland. Carlton Cole headed his side into the lead before Kenwyne Jones levelled shortly after the break. A late double substitution of Luis Boa Morte and Nolberto Solano proved decisive as the latter forced £9m keeper Craig Gordon to fumble the ball into his own net. Craig Bellamy added a third in injury time but the result came courtesy of some hard work at the other end as well. Robert Green produced a fine save to deny Grant Leadbitter shortly after Jones' equaliser.

Green was the hero again the following week in the closing stages of West Ham United's goalless draw against Portsmouth at Fratton Park. Harry Redknapp's men were awarded a penalty in the dying minutes of injury time for a Danny Gabbidon handball, but Green held his nerve to keep Benjani's spot-kick out and earn a point for the Hammers.

Three days later a cold night in Coventry proved nervy for West Ham United's Carling Cup aspirations. Jay Tabb put the home side ahead with a header before Luis Boa Morte levelled late on. Carlton Cole fired the Hammers into the quarter-finals deep into injury time.

10 facts about
Craig Bellamy

He was born in Canton in Cardiff.

Craig is actually his middle name.

He had a trial at Bradford City but the club didn't take him on and he went and joined the youth team at Norwich City instead.

He set up his own football academy for disadvantaged children in Sierra Leone.

His favourite TV shows are EastEnders and Only Fools and Horses.

He can't stand olives.

His favourite type of food is Japanese.

His all-time hero is the boxer Oscar De La Hoya.

He was voted into the Norwich City Hall of Fame in 2002.

He has captained Wales since June 2007.

November 2007

04 November 2007 - Barclays Premier League

West Ham United   1   Bolton Wanderers   1

McCartney 20   Nolan 90

Attendance: 33,867

10 November 2007 - Barclays Premier League

Derby County   0   West Ham United   5

Bowyer 42, 59   Etherington 51   Lewis (OG) 55   Solano 69

Attendance: 32,440

25 November 2007 - Barclays Premier League

West Ham United   1   Tottenham Hotspur   1

Cole 20   Dawson 67

Attendance: 34,966

George McCartney fired West Ham United into a successful November with his first-ever goal for the club. The Northern Ireland international struck in the 20th minute with a spectacular volley to put the home side ahead against Bolton Wanderers but the visitors were determined to steal a share of the spoils. Wanderers struck the woodwork twice before Kevin Nolan netted an equaliser in the dying seconds of the game.

Fired up from the late frustrations of the previous week, Alan Curbishley's men travelled to Pride Park for a result which equalled the club's record win margin away from home in the top flight – 6-1 against Manchester City in September 1962. Lee Bowyer scored a goal in each half as the Hammers cruised to a 5-0 victory and assisted Matty Etherington in scoring another. Following an own goal, Nolberto Solano confirmed the rout with a perfectly-placed free-kick.

Later in the month, rivals Tottenham Hotspur were the visitors to the Boleyn Ground. Carlton Cole secured the goal his recent performances had merited before Spurs defender Michael Dawson levelled midway through the second half. A point apiece seemed the likely outcome until Jermain Defoe tumbled under Lucas Neill's challenge in added time and referee Mike Riley pointed to the penalty spot.

Robert Green again saved the day – and his third penalty of the season – to deny Defoe and ensure a well-earned draw for the Hammers.

December 2007

01 December 2007 - Barclays Premier League

Chelsea 1   West Ham United 0

J Cole 76

Attendance: 41,830

09 December 2007 - Barclays Premier League

Blackburn Rovers 0   West Ham United 1

Ashton 52

Attendance: 20,870

12 December 2007 - Carling Cup quarter-final

West Ham United 1   Everton 2

Cole 12   Osman 40   Yakubu 88

Attendance: 28,777

15 December 2007 - Barclays Premier League

West Ham United 0   Everton 2

Yakubu 45   Johnson 90

Attendance: 34,430

22 December 2007 - Barclays Premier League

Middlesbrough 1   West Ham United 2

Wheater 40   Ashton 44   Parker 90

Attendance: 26,007

26 December 2007 - Barclays Premier League

West Ham United 1   Reading 1

Solano 42   Kitson 60

Attendance: 34,227

29 December 2007 - Barclays Premier League

West Ham United 2   Manchester United 1

Ronaldo 14   Ferdinand 77   Upson 82

Attendance: 34,966

A stunning solitary strike from former Hammer Joe Cole subjected West Ham United to their first defeat in six games at the beginning of December as Chelsea confirmed at 1-0 victory at Stamford Bridge. A long trip to Lancashire was next for Alan Curbishley's men, this time a single goal from in-form Dean Ashton propelled the Hammers back into the top half of the table with a win against Blackburn Rovers.

Two games in quick succession against David Moyes' high-flying Everton side swiftly followed; the first a crucial Carling Cup quarter-final at the Boleyn Ground. Carlton Cole scored his fourth of the season to take an early lead but Leon Osman levelled five minutes before the break. Ayegbeni Yakubu snuffed out the Hammers' dreams of League Cup silverware in the 88th minute, taking advantage of a defensive mix-up to slot home the winner.

Moyes' men scored another two when Saturday came around, this time in the Barclays Premier League. Yakubu snatched a goal on the stroke of half-time and Andy Johnson added a second in the closing minutes of the game.

The crowded fixture schedule took the Hammers up to Middlesbrough on the Saturday before Christmas where David Wheater put the home side ahead. But West Ham United's response was emphatic and Ashton levelled toward the end of the first half before Scott Parker's impressive solo effort in the 90th minute secured all three points. Reading were next to the Boleyn Ground on Boxing Day where Nolberto Solano gave the hosts an interval lead but Dave Kitson equalised with a crisp finish on the hour.

Title holders Manchester United visited three days later for the final fixture of 2007. Cristiano Ronaldo gave the visitors the lead in the first half but failed to double the lead midway through the second. The Portuguese winger misplaced his spot-kick – awarded for a Jonathan Spector handball – and fired wide as Green maintained his season-long unbeaten run from the penalty spot.

The miss was to prove crucial as two finishes from West Ham United's two centre-backs followed in a five minute spell. First Anton Ferdinand sent a thumping header past Tomasz Kuszczak from Mark Noble's corner, then in the 82nd minute Matty Upson nodded in Noble's precision free-kick as the Hammers recorded another victory against the Premier League champions.

January 2008

01 January 2008 - Barclays Premier League
Arsenal   2   West Ham United   0
Eduardo 2   Adebayor 18
Attendance: 60,102

05 January 2008 - FA Cup third round
West Ham United   0   Manchester City   0
Attendance: 33,806

12 January 2008 - Barclays Premier League
West Ham United   2   Fulham   1
Ashton 28   Davies 8   Ferdinand 69
Attendance: 34,947

16 January 2008 - FA Cup third round replay
Manchester City   1   West Ham United   0
Elano 73
Attendance: 27,809

20 January 2008 - Barclays Premier League
Manchester City   1   West Ham United   1
Cole 8   Vassell 16
Attendance: 39,042

30 January 2008 - Barclays Premier League
West Ham United   1   Liverpool   0
Noble 90 (pen)
Attendance: 34,977

Arsenal forward Eduardo was quick to get off the mark in 2008, firing the Gunners ahead after just two minutes at the Emirates stadium. Young midfielder Jack Collison made his debut for the Hammers, replacing the injured Freddie Ljungberg, but Arsene Wenger's side were too hot to handle and a goal from Emmanuel Adebayor rounded off the scoring.

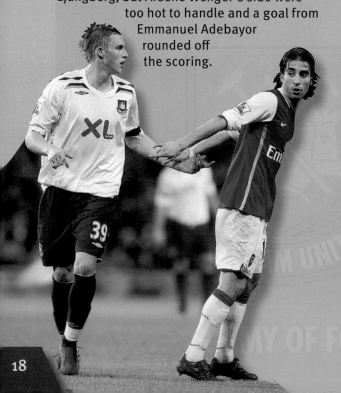

Four days later and West Ham United faced the first of three January encounters against Manchester City. The FA Cup third round tie was a closely-fought encounter at the Boleyn Ground. Both Robert Green and City goalkeeper Joe Hart were in fine form to keep the scoreline blank.

Relegation-threatened Fulham were next to the Boleyn Ground, breaking up the trio of Manchester City matches. Simon Davies put the visitors ahead early on before Dean Ashton levelled on the half-hour mark. Anton Ferdinand sweetly finished Mark Noble's cut-back to secure all three points.

The first of two successive trips to Eastlands followed, with Elano ensuring Manchester City made it through to the fourth round of the FA Cup – his late strike breaking the 163-minute-long deadlock between the two sides. The Hammers were keen to make an instant impact on their return to the City of Manchester stadium four days later and Carlton Cole struck early to put them in the driving seat. But Darius Vassell claimed the equaliser less than ten minutes later and the points were shared.

The final game of the month took place under the floodlights at the Boleyn Ground with Liverpool the visitors. The game had looked like it would end goalless until Jamie Carragher's added-time foul on Freddie Ljungberg left referee Alan Wiley pointing to the penalty spot. Mark Noble held his nerve to fire past Jose Reina and seal the victory for West Ham United.

February 2008

02 February 2008 - Barclays Premier League

Wigan Athletic 1   **West Ham United** 0

Kilbane 45

Attendance: 20,525

09 February 2008 - Barclays Premier League

West Ham United 1   **Birmingham City** 1

Ljungberg 7   McFadden 16 (pen)

Attendance: 34,884

23 February 2008 - Barclays Premier League

Fulham 0   **West Ham United** 1

Solano 87

Attendance: 25,280

February began with West Ham United in tenth position in the league – just two points behind Portsmouth. The team travelled up to Wigan to take on Steve Bruce's side, but found the going tough on the Latics' mud-ridden pitch.

Kevin Kilbane struck just before half-time with a looping header in what proved to be the only goal of the game as both teams' attacking inventions were stifled by the conditions.

West Ham United centre-back Matthew Upson earned a call-up to Fabio Capello's first England squad in the week leading up to the visit of his former club, Birmingham City, to the Boleyn Ground. Upson played the full 90 minutes for his country in a 2-1 victory against Switzerland, three days

before Alex McLeish's Blues descended on Upton Park. Freddie Ljungberg scored his first Premier League goal for the Hammers inside the first ten minutes only for James McFadden to equalise on the quarter-hour mark from the penalty spot – the first spot-kick of the season to pass Robert Green. His low penalty brushed the keeper's outstretched glove.

A break for FA Cup action ensued, leaving West Ham United to prepare for a trip across London to Fulham. Both teams honoured the 15th anniversary of Bobby Moore's passing before kick-off on a chilly afternoon in west London.

As the tough contest edge towards a goalless conclusion, despite chances for both sides, Green made an excellent save to keep Jimmy Bullard from putting Fulham in front after 86 minutes. The stop proved crucial as the visitors mounted a counter-attack and Nolberto Solano coolly finished Luis Boa Morte's knock-down to ensure an away win for the Hammers.

March 2008

01 March 2008 - Barclays Premier League

West Ham United 0   **Chelsea** 4

Lampard 17 (pen)   J Cole 20   Ballack 22   A Cole 64

Attendance: 34,969

05 March 2008 - Barclays Premier League

Liverpool 4   **West Ham United** 0

Torres 8, 61, 81   Gerrard 83

Attendance: 42,954

09 March 2008 - Barclays Premier League

Tottenham Hotspur 4   **West Ham United** 0

Berbatov 8, 11   Gilberto 85   Bent 90

Attendance: 36,062

15 March 2008 - Barclays Premier League

West Ham United 2   **Blackburn Rovers** 1

Santa Cruz 19   Ashton 39   Sears 81

Attendance: 34,006

22 March 2008 - Barclays Premier League

Everton 1   **West Ham United** 1

Yakubu 8   Ashton 68

Attendance: 37,430

29 March 2008 - Barclays Premier League

Sunderland 2   **West Ham United** 1

Ljungberg 18   Jones 29   Reid 90

Attendance: 45,690

March began with a succession of freak results for West Ham United, beginning with the first of three 4-0 defeats at home to Chelsea. Frank Lampard struck early on for the visitors from the penalty spot before seeing red for a challenge on Luis Boa Morte. Joe Cole and Michael Ballack were next on the score sheet as Chelsea scored three in 5 minutes. Ashley Cole added the fourth with just under an hour left to play.

The second 4-0 of the month came at Anfield as Fernando Torres displayed fine form to hit a hat-trick for Liverpool in a fixture rearranged due to the Merseysiders' Champions League commitments. Steven Gerrard scored the fourth in trademark sublime style.

The Hammers travelled to White Hart Lane next and conceded twice in the first 15 minutes from Dimitar Berbatov finishing off set plays provided by Tom Huddlestone. Gilberto and Darren Bent added the third and fourth to round off the scoring in the final ten minutes.

With bets being laid on a fourth successive 4-0 defeat, the Hammers responded with class and style to record a 2-1 win over visiting Blackburn Rovers. Roque Santa Cruz fired Rovers into the lead but Dean Ashton levelled before the break. All eyes were on debutant Freddie Sears – a second half substitute – who repaid the manager's faith and headed in the winner.

Another trip to Liverpool followed – this time to take on Europe-chasing Everton, who took an early lead through Ayegbeni Yakubu shortly after James Tomkins hit the woodwork on his full debut. Dean Ashton popped up with the equaliser for the visiting Hammers midway through the second half.

Struggling Sunderland were the final opponents of the month and West Ham United were in front after 18 minutes through Freddie Ljungberg. But the Black Cats showed their spirit which secured them Premier League survival and won out with a goal from Kenwyne Jones and an added-time finish from midfielder Andy Reid.

21

April 2008

08 April 2008 - Barclays Premier League

West Ham United   0   **Portsmouth**   1

Kranjcar 61

Attendance: 33,629

12 April 2008 - Barclays Premier League

Bolton Wanderers   1   **West Ham United**   0

Davies 47

Attendance: 23,043

19 April 2008 - Barclays Premier League

West Ham United   2   **Derby County**   1

Zamora 20   Mears 65   Cole 77

Attendance: 34,612

26 April 2008 - Barclays Premier League

West Ham United   2   **Newcastle United**   2

Noble 10   Ashton 23   Martins 42   Geremi 45

Attendance: 34,980

Many eyes in England were on the Champions League semi-final between Arsenal and Liverpool as West Ham United played host to Portsmouth in a fixture rearranged to accommodate their FA Cup commitments. It proved to be a close contest, but Pompey edged the victory with a goal from Niko Kranjcar just after the hour mark.

The Hammers faced a Bolton Wanderers side battling relegation at the Reebok Stadium and the first half ended goalless. Kevin Davies capitalised on a fortunate bounce in the penalty area to score early in the second and clinch all three points.

Relegated Derby County were next to the Boleyn Ground but West Ham United put on an assured display, despite the Rams' battling performance. Bobby Zamora secured the lead before former Hammer Tyrone Mears scored the equaliser. Carlton Cole grabbed the deserving winner for the home side with just over ten minutes left.

Kevin Keegan's buoyant Newcastle United side travelled to Upton Park next but West Ham United were in fine fettle. Mark Noble's sublime half-volley was swiftly followed by Dean Ashton's low-angled shot past Steve Harper in a goal-packed first half. Obafemi Martins and Geremi added their names to the scoresheet before the break to secure a 2-2 draw.

10 facts about
Dean Ashton

He was born in Swindon, Wiltshire.

He came to prominence at Crewe Alexandra
after coming through their school of excellence
under long-serving manager Dario Gradi.

His has a son called Ethan.

His worst habit is biting his nails.

He can't stand the thought
of eating oysters.

The best away ground he says
he's played at is the Emirates.

He wears three socks on
his right foot and two on
his left in every game.

His favourite TV
show is Ramsay's
Kitchen Nightmares.

His favourite film is Man on Fire.

He could have had trials
for England to compete in the
discus when he was at school
but he opted to play football.

03 May 2008 - Barclays Premier League
Manchester United 4 **West Ham United** 1
Ronaldo 3, 24 Tevez 26 Ashton 28 Carrick 59
Attendance: 76,013

11 May 2008 - Barclays Premier League
West Ham United 2 **Aston Villa** 2
Solano 8 Young 14 Barry 58 Ashton 88
Attendance: 34,969

An early kick-off at sun-drenched Old Trafford was the setting for West Ham United's penultimate game of the season and it transpired to be a lively opening half-hour. Player of the Year Cristiano Ronaldo scored a brace inside 25 minutes with former Hammer of the Year Carlos Tevez making it 3-0 two minutes later. Dean Ashton pulled a goal back in spectacular style with an overhead kick before Nani was sent off for a headbutt on skipper Lucas Neill. Another former Hammer, Michael Carrick, rounded off the scoring with just over an hour left on the clock.

Aston Villa were the visitors for the final fixture of the 2007/08 campaign and Nolberto Solano fired the opener past his former club after just 8 minutes. Villa, who were still in contention for a Uefa Cup spot going into the game, equalised through Ashley Young before Gareth Barry put them ahead in the 58th minute. Dean Ashton had the final say as he netted to minutes from time to secure the 2-2 draw.

Club Honours

European Cup Winners' Cup
Winners: 1964/65
Runners-up: 1975/76

FA Cup
Winners: 1963/64, 1974/75, 1979/80
Runners-up: 1922/23, 2005/06

League Cup
Runners-up: 1965/66, 1980/81

UEFA Intertoto Cup
Winners: 1999

**Football League
Championship Play-off**
Winners: 2005

**Football League Division Two
(now Championship)**
Winners: 1957/58, 1980/81
Runners-up: 1922/23, 1990/91, 1992/93
(as renamed Division One)

Football League War Cup
Winners: 1939/40

Charity Shield
Winners (joint): 1964

FA Youth Cup
Winners: 1962/63, 1980/81, 1998/99

Player Profiles

Robert Green

Nationality: English
Date of Birth: 18/01/1980
Previous clubs: Norwich City
Position: Goalkeeper

Robert arrived at the Boleyn Ground at the beginning of the 2006/07 campaign after spending ten years at Norwich City. While he was there he helped the Canaries win promotion to the Premier League in 2004 and was rewarded with a call-up to the England squad, but a groin injury suffered during an international friendly cost him his place in the squad for the 2006 World Cup. In 2007 he established himself as West Ham United's number one and was a key figure in the team's memorable end of 2006/07 season winning run, with notably outstanding performances against Arsenal and Manchester United. He became the fifth goalkeeper to win the Hammer of the Year award at the end of the 2007/08 season.

Marek Stech

Nationality: Czech
Date of Birth: 28/01/1990
Previous clubs: AC Sparta Praha
Position: Goalkeeper

Goalkeeping coach Ludek Miklosko has high hopes for his compatriot Marek and his form for the West Ham United youth and reserve sides underlined that before he signed a five-year contract in July 2008. He joined the club two years previously having made waves for the Czech Republic at youth level. At 6'4, Stech is an imposing figure but he is quiet and modest off the pitch and is extremely popular with his team-mates. Highly ambitious, he aspires to achieve the success of Petr Cech.

Jimmy Walker

Nationality: English
Date of Birth: 09/07/1973
Previous clubs: Walsall, Notts County
Position: Goalkeeper

Like former Hammers favourite Phil Parkes, Jimmy also arrived at the Boleyn Ground from Walsall and the hugely popular goalkeeper established himself as a fans' favourite in east London, following his signing in summer 2004. An outstanding professional, Jimmy also has a reputation as a practical joker, thanks to his matchday programme column in which he spills the beans on the dressing room antics and takes the mickey out of his team-mates. He became a local legend during his eleven years with Walsall, too, after joining the Midlanders on a free transfer from the Notts County youth ranks in August 1993.

Lucas Neill

Nationality: Australian
Date of Birth: 09/03/1978
Previous clubs: Millwall, Blackburn Rovers
Position: Defender

The Australia captain turned down an offer from Liverpool to join West Ham United from Blackburn Rovers for an undisclosed fee in January 2007. His immediate influence in the dressing room was widely regarded as one of the key factors in the club's successful battle for survival that season. Born in Sydney, Lucas was registered on a football scholarship with the Australian Institute of Sport after leaving college in 1994. At 17, he moved to London in November 1995 and spent six years at Millwall before stepping up another level to the Premiership, signing for newly-promoted Blackburn in a £1m deal.

George McCartney

Nationality: Northern Irish
Date of Birth: 29/04/1981
Previous clubs: Sunderland
Position: Defender

George was runner-up in the Hammer of the Year award at the end of the 2007/8 season thanks to his consistent performances at left-back. He signed from Sunderland in a deal worth £1m in August 2006. West Ham United paid the Black Cats £600,000 and added defender Clive Clarke to the package in order to secure the services of the Northern Ireland international, who had progressed through the youth ranks at the Stadium of Light to become club captain. After making his debut in the League Cup against Luton Town in September 2000, George went on to make 157 league and cup appearances for the Wearsiders.

Daniel Gabbidon

Nationality: Welsh
Date of Birth: 08/08/1979 Height
Previous clubs: West Bromwich Albion, Cardiff City
Position: Defender

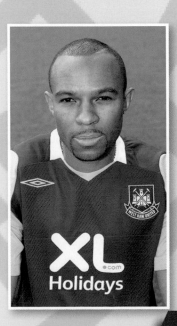

The Hammer of the Year winner in 2006, Danny sadly had to spend much of the 2007/08 season on the sidelines with an abdominal injury. The Welsh international joined West Ham United alongside James Collins in August 2005. The defensive duo had met up at Cardiff City, where they became solid figures in the heart of the Bluebirds rearguard, before being reluctantly released by the Ninian Park outfit for an undisclosed fee. Danny began his career as a schoolboy at West Bromwich Albion, and went on to make 20 league appearances for the club before being transferred to Cardiff for £175,000 in August 2000.

Matthew Etherington

Nationality: English
Date of Birth: 14/08/1981
Previous clubs: Peterborough United, Bradford City (loan), Tottenham Hotspur Position: Midfielder

One of West Ham United's longest-serving players, Matthew originally graduated through the junior ranks at Peterborough United, where he made his debut at Brentford in May 1997, aged just 15 years and 262 days. After establishing himself at London Road during the 1998/99 campaign, he made a £500,000 move to Tottenham Hotspur in January 2000. He made his Tottenham debut as a substitute at Liverpool in April 2000, before going to Bradford City for a 13-match loan spell in autumn 2001. Going into the 2007/08 season, having scored 13 goals in 158 appearances for the Hammers, the refreshed winger looked determined to rediscover the form that made him such a hit when he first arrived at the Boleyn Ground and this was underlined in September 2007 by a match-winning double-strike at Reading.

Carlton Cole

Nationality: English
Date of Birth: 12/10/1983
Previous clubs: Wolverhampton Wanderers (loan), Aston Villa (loan), Charlton Athletic (loan), Chelsea
Position: Striker

The former England Under-21 striker, capped 19 times by his country at that level, signed from Premier League champions Chelsea in July 2006 to add further firepower to the West Ham United front line. A product of the youth academy system at Stamford Bridge, he was handed his first team debut for the Blues as an 18-year-old substitute against Everton in April 2002 and then he scored on his first start for Claudio Ranieri at Middlesbrough. Carlton then headed to Alan Curbishley's Charlton Athletic for a year-long loan stint at The Valley, where he struck five goals in 22 appearances for the Addicks during the 2003/04 campaign. He has continued to improve under Curbishley at West Ham United and cement his place in the Hammers side.

Tony Stokes

Nationality: English
Date of Birth: 07/01/1987
Previous clubs: Rushden and Diamonds (loan), Brighton and Hove Albion (loan), Stevenage Borough (loan)
Position: Midfielder

Tony Stokes is a combative but creative midfielder with an eye for goal who has impressed in coming through West Ham United's youth ranks in recent years. He made his first-team debut in September 2005 as a substitute in a League Cup match against Sheffield Wednesday. He then spent time later that season on loan at Rushden and Diamonds, playing 19 times. Another loan followed in August 2006 at Brighton and Hove Albion that saw him get six league games under his belt. Stokes returned to the Boleyn Ground and produced some solid reserve-team displays early in the 2007/08 season. He went on loan to Conference side Stevenage Borough in November 2007. Upon his return to West Ham United for the closing stages of the campaign, Stokes regained the reserve-team captaincy he had previously held with Jack Collison's emergence. He also more than impressed in the end of season tour to the Hong Kong soccer sevens, scoring several goals and leading a youthful team. Stokes agreed another one-year deal at the end of the campaign.

Mark Noble

Nationality: English
Date of Birth: 08/05/1987
Previous clubs: Ipswich Town (loan), Hull City (loan)
Position: Midfielder

This highly-rated homegrown talent simply goes from strength to strength in the heart of the West Ham United midfield. The former Woodside and Royal Docks schoolboy was initially snapped up by Arsenal as a kid but the Canning Town youngster's first love was always the Hammers and he was a regular spectator at the Boleyn Ground with his claret and blue-blooded family. After quitting the Gunners in favour of the Hammers, he progressed through the youth ranks and, aged 15, became the youngest-ever player to appear in the club's reserve team in February 2003. Having been involved with the first-team squad on several occasions, Alan Pardew handed him his first-team debut aged 17 years and 108 days, as a substitute in the 2-0 League Cup victory over Southend United in August 2004.

Hayden Mullins

Nationality: English
Date of Birth: 27/03/1979
Previous clubs: Crystal Palace
Position: Midfielder

The three-times capped England Under-21 midfielder arrived at the Boleyn Ground in October 2003, ending his six-year spell at Selhurst Park, where he had played 256 league and cup matches, scoring 18 goals. The Reading-born midfielder made his West Ham United debut in a 1-1 draw against Nottingham Forest in October 2003 but his dream of making it to the promised land of the Premier League was shattered 33 matches later in the Championship play-off final at the Millennium Stadium by his former club Crystal Palace. A year later, Hayden was back in Cardiff helping the club into the top-flight with a play-off final victory over Preston North End and went on to play an influential role in the barnstorming late run to Premier League survival in 2006/07.

Jonathan Spector

Nationality: American
Date of Birth: 01/03/1986
Previous clubs: Charlton Athletic (loan), Manchester United
Position: Defender

The versatile United States defender joined West Ham United in a £500,000 move from Manchester United on 15 June 2006 and has been an important member of the squad ever since. Born and raised in Arlington Heights, a suburb of Chicago, Jonathan moved to England at the age of 17 to join United in the summer of 2003 and made his senior debut just a year later, in the Community Shield against Arsenal at the Millennium Stadium. He went on to make seven league and cup appearances for Sir Alex Ferguson's side in the 2004/05 campaign, including two in the Champions League against Dinamo Bucharest and Fenerbahce. In November 2004, he made his full international debut, as a substitute in a World Cup qualifier against Jamaica.

James Collins

Nationality: Welsh
Date of Birth: 23/08/1983
Previous clubs: Cardiff City
Position: Defender

James has represented Wales at every level and scorched on to the scene, aged 17, when he was handed his Cardiff debut in an FA Cup first round tie against Bristol Rovers in November 2000. A powerful player, who is virtually unbeatable in the air, Collins' style was key to the Hammers strength at the back and his performances were crucial in the race to achieve Premier League survival at the end of the 2006/07 season. He suffered a major setback in a January 2008 reserve-team match away to Portsmouth, suffering cruciate ligament damage to his right knee that sidelined him for the rest of the campaign.

Julien Faubert

Nationality: French
Date of Birth: 01/08/1983
Previous clubs: Cannes, Bordeaux
Position: Midfielder

Born in Le Havre, Julien headed south in 1998 when he was offered a place at the AS Cannes youth academy, famous for nurturing such talents as Zinedine Zidane, Johan Micoud and Patrick Vieira. He went on to make 45 senior appearances for the Cote d'Azur club before moving to Bordeaux in September 2004. The fast and powerful midfielder earned a call-up to the French national squad following the 2006 World Cup finals and became the first player to wear the famous number ten shirt following the retirement of Zinedine Zidane. He moved across the Channel in July 2007 but his first season at the Boleyn Ground was hampered by suffering an achilles injury in pre-season which ruled him out for six months.

Kyel Reid

Nationality: English
Date of Birth: 26/11/1987
Previous clubs: Barnsley (loan), Crystal Palace (loan)
Position: Midfielder

Another youth academy product, Kyel Reid is a skilful left winger who has played internationally for England Under-19s. He made his full debut for West Ham United in May 2006 in a 1-0 win away to West Bromwich Albion. He has enjoyed a loan spell at Barnsley, where he made 26 appearances and scored two goals in the 2006/07 season. In the 2007/08 season he made four league and cup appearances for West Ham United, firstly in the League Cup third round where his well-timed cross set Dean Ashton up to score a last-gasp winner against Plymouth Argyle. He joined Crystal Palace on loan until the end of the season in March 2008.

Nigel Quashie

Nationality: Scottish
Date of Birth: 20/07/1978
Previous clubs: West Bromwich Albion, Portsmouth, Southampton, Nottingham Forest, Queens Park Rangers
Position: Midfielder

The Scottish international became Alan Curbishley's second signing when he completed a £1.5m move from West Bromwich Albion in January 2007.That transfer signalled a welcome return to his London roots for Surrey-born Nigel, who had made his Queens Park Rangers debut as a 17-year-old against Manchester United at Old Trafford in December 1995, before going on to score five goals in 63 outings for the Loftus Road club. During that time, Quashie also won four England Under-21 caps. His Hammers career was put on hold after he suffered a foot injury during a game against Tottenham Hotspur in March 2007.

Lee Bowyer

Nationality: English
Date of Birth: 03/01/1977
Previous clubs: Newcastle United, Charlton Athletic, Leeds United
Position: Midfielder

Growing up as a West Ham United fan, Lee's boyhood hero was Billy Bonds and just like the Hammers legend he also started his career as a schoolboy at Charlton Athletic. He made impressive progress at youth level, before going on to score 14 goals in 58 league and cup outings for the Addicks. He had made his debut as a 17-year-old substitute in a League Cup second round second-leg defeat by Swindon Town in September 1994. The once-capped England midfielder became a West Ham United player for the second time when he returned to the Boleyn Ground from Newcastle United in June 2006. Raised in nearby Poplar, Lee had previously made eleven appearances for the club after signing on a short-term contract from Leeds United in January 2003. He has been an influential player at West Ham United ever since his return and hopes to remain until the end of his career.

James Tomkins

Nationality: English
Date of Birth: 29/03/1989
Position: Defender

Basildon-born James is a ball-playing central defender who is as comfortable in possession as he is rising above attackers to clear his lines. The tall and imposing youth academy product endured a frustrating stop-start time in the 2006/07 season after two shoulder injuries but battled back to fitness by October of the following campaign. A fine display in the 1-0 reserve-team win against Tottenham Hotspur suggested that he was close to recapturing his best form and, alongside Jack Collison and Freddie Sears, began to capture the attention of Alan Curbishley. He made his first-team debut on 22 March 2008 when he played the full 90 minutes of a 1-1 draw at Everton, In all, making five starts and one substitute appearance at the end of the 2007/08 season.

Kieron Dyer

Nationality: English
Date of Birth: 29/12/1978
Previous clubs: Newcastle United, Ipswich Town
Position: Midfielder

The England international became a West Ham United player in the summer of 2007 and turned in some impressive performances before disaster struck just three games into the season. Just six days after winning his 33rd England cap against Germany, he suffered a double fracture of his right leg in the League Cup second round tie at Bristol Rovers, which ruled him out of the remainder of the 2007/08 campaign. The Ipswich-born livewire originally joined his hometown club as a schoolboy and won England youth caps before making his debut on Boxing Day 1996 in a 3-1 win against Crystal Palace. After scoring a dozen goals in 113 league and cup outings for the Portman Road side, the eleven-times capped England Under-21 international was snapped up by Newcastle United for £6.5m in July 1999 where he went on to score 36 goals in 251 league and cup games for the Magpies.

Luis Boa Morte

Nationality: Portuguese
Date of Birth: 04/08/1977
Previous clubs: Sporting Lisbon, Fulham, Southampton, Arsenal
Position: Striker

The Portuguese international was Alan Curbishley's first signing as West Ham United manager when he joined from Fulham in January 2007 and he scored his first goal for the club in the crucial 3-0 win at relegation-rivals Wigan Athletic three months later. The Boleyn Ground became Luis' third London home, after he had previously enjoyed spells at Highbury and Craven Cottage. Boa Morte - whose surname literally translates as 'Good Death' - began his professional career as a left winger with his hometown club, Sporting Lisbon. He was then spotted by Arsenal manager Arsene Wenger representing his country in an Under-21 tournament and had a dream start to Premier League life, winning a title medal during his first year at Highbury. On the international front, he was called into the Portuguese squad that beat England on their way to the 2006 World Cup semi-finals in Germany.

Calum Davenport

Nationality: English
Date of Birth: 01/01/1983
Previous clubs: Coventry City, Norwich City (loan), Watford (loan), Southampton (loan), Tottenham Hotspur
Position: Defender

Calum arrived at the Boleyn Ground in January 2007 to bolster the defence in the crucial run-in to the end of season. Unfortunately, injury ruled him out for the season after just half-a-dozen outings, but he was looking to get back on track during the 2007/08 campaign and was fit again by October. He was loaned to Watford for an initial one-month deal but he fractured a bone in his neck on his Hornets debut on 19 January, an injury which would sideline him for some time. Born in Bedford, the eight-times capped England Under-21 international joined Aston Villa as a 12-year-old schoolboy before moving to Derby County. He then began his professional career at Coventry City after progressing through the youth ranks at Highfield Road, where he was twice an FA Youth Cup runner-up.

Holmar Orn Eyjolfsson

Nationality: Icelandic
Date of Birth: 06/08/1990
Previous clubs: HK Kopavogur
Position: Defender

Holmar first spent a week on trial at Chadwell Heath back in February 2008 having caught the eye as he rapidly rose through the Icelandic youth ranks. Eyjolfsson, who featured regularly for HK since making his debut at the age of 16, then moved permanently to the Boleyn Ground in July 2008. Already capped at Under-21 level by his country, the versatile defender, who can also play in midfield, is bidding to follow in the footsteps of his father Eyjólfur Gjafar Sverrisson - a former Icelandic international who enjoyed an illustrious playing career in Germany and Turkey.

Valon Behrami

Nationality: Swiss
Date of Birth: 19/04/1985
Previous clubs: Lugano, Genoa, Verona, Lazio
Position: Defender

A tireless performer, versatile Valon was a prized capture for West Ham United when he put pen to paper at the end of July 2008. The Kosovan-born player's rise to prominence in his adopted Switzerland, and then in the rarefied air of Serie A in Italy, earned him a reputation across Europe. He cemented his growing stature with a memorable derby winner for Lazio against Roma in March 2008. He then went on to feature for the host nation at the European Championship, having already got a taste of the World Cup and also appeared in the Champions League with Lazio.

Jan Lastuvka

Nationality: Czech
Date of Birth: 07/07/1982
Previous Clubs: Fulham (loan), Shakhtar Donetsk
Position: Goalkeeper

A former Under-21 international, Lastuvka spent four years at goalkeeping coach Ludek Miklosko's former club Banik Ostrava, including winning the Czech title in the 2003/04 season. He then moved on to Ukrainian football. He joined West Ham United in July 2008 on a one-year loan from Ukrainian club Shakhtar Donetsk.

10 facts about
Matthew Etherington

He was born in Truro, Cornwall.

He made his league debut at the age of 15 for Peterborough United.

His all-time hero is his granddad.

He admits that his worst habit is sleeping too much.

He loves Dairy Milk chocolate.

If he hadn't been a footballer he would have been a PE teacher.

His most treasured possession is his mobile phone.

His favourite place in the world is Cornwall.

He loves watching 24 and Friends.

He thinks Lee Bowyer is the worst dressed player at West Ham United.

All about....
Herbie the Hammer

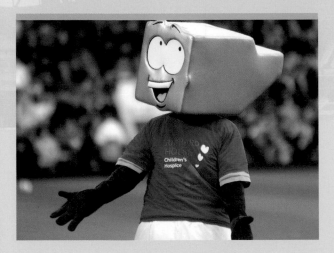

A familiar figure at the Boleyn Ground on matchdays, Herbie the Hammer is West Ham United's biggest fan and is always on hand to get the crowd cheering – but how did he come to be our mascot...?

The story goes that many moons ago, Molly the tea lady was drifting off to sleep after a long day's work one Saturday at the Boleyn Ground when she heard a loud banging noise and went to investigate.

She found five dustbins in the players' tunnel, all in a row, which was very unusual. Suddenly, out popped a living, breathing hammer! He had been hiding in his secret home in the tunnels under the Boleyn Ground.

Herbie's great-grandfather had lived at the Iron Works after his family moved from Mascot Land but they had all made the underground tunnels at Upton Park their new home when he was a baby.

At night he would play his dustbin drums to keep himself amused but, most of all, he liked to keep an eye on the football matches from a secret viewing hole in one of the tunnels. When Molly found that out she suggested that West Ham United adopt Herbie – which they did without hesitation – and he happily became the biggest Hammer in the land...

Make sure you give Herbie a big wave the next time you see him!

USA & Canada Summer Tour

USA – 18 July-21 July

20 July 2008 (Crew Stadium, Columbus)

Columbus Crew   1-3   **West Ham United**

Garey 20   Ashton 6   Evans (og) 26   Reid 52

The hard work in training left Alan Curbishley in upbeat mood for the friendly

Craig Bellamy's hard work beforehand was to pay off with a man of the match display

Julien Faubert got stuck in despite the soaring temperatures

Jonathan Spector was a welcome visitor despite missing out on the tour in his homeland

Dean Ashton earned the plaudits after opening the scoring with a great goal

The travelling fans were out in great numbers for a rousing contest

Carlton Cole helped play his part as West Ham United hung on for the win

38

CANADA – 21-25 July 2008

24 July 2008 (BMO Field, Toronto)

MLS All-Stars	3-2	West Ham United
Gomez 27 Blanco 44		Ashton 26, 67
De Rosario (pen) 70		

Media interest was high before the game with club captain Lucas Neill among those in demand

With a sell-out crowd and a world TV audience, it was a spectacular occasion

The famous CN Tower in the distance provided a fitting backdrop

Dean Ashton scored twice but the All-Stars just edged it in five-goal thriller

Cuauhtémoc Blanco, up against Scott Parker here, was the MLS hero

Luis Boa Morte had a late chance to ensure a draw but was just denied

Young Joe Widdowson had a game to remember marking David Beckham

39

10 facts about
Robert Green

His middle name is Paul.

He made his debut in a local derby between Norwich City and Ipswich Town and kept a clean sheet.

He spent ten years at Norwich City before joining West Ham United in the summer of 2006.

He grew up in Surrey.

He has an eight foot painting of Alan Partridge on his wall at home.

He writes a column for the Independent newspaper.

His favourite TV programme is The Simpsons.

He can't stomach bananas but likes eating sushi.

He supports Woking FC.

His favourite board game is Boggle.

Crossword

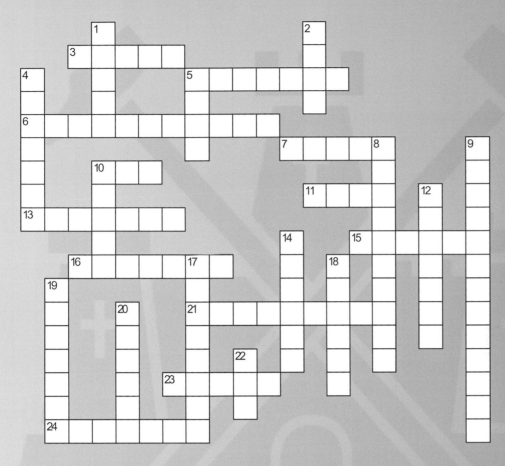

Down

1 He scored the Hammers' first goal of the 2007/08 season (5)

2 First name of former players Gayle and Cottee (4)

4 Carlton Cole's position on the pitch (7)

5 Tony _____, director of the youth academy (4)

8 George McCartney's former club (10)

9 West Ham United's official colours (6,3,4)

10 Ashton's nickname (5)

12 The fans' favourite song (7)

14 First name of West Ham United's left-back (6)

17 _____ Heath, where the Hammers train (8)

18 _____ Ground, West Ham's home (6)

19 First name of defender _____Upson (7)

20 Bristol _____, West Ham United knocked them out of the Carling Cup in August 2007 (6)

22 Anton's older brother (3)

Across

3 Bobby _____, West Ham United legend (5)

5 Mark Noble was born in _____ Town (7)

6 Hammer of the Year 2007/08 (6,5)

7 Jack Collison's national team (5)

10 Last name of the assistant manager (3)

11 The first name of the ex-Hammers' boss (4)

13 Cristiano _____, Manchester United player who missed a penalty at the Boleyn Ground in December 2007 (7)

15 West Ham United's Hammer-shaped mascot (6)

16 Dean Ashton's former club (7)

21 Lucas Neill's country of origin (9)

23 First name of the reserve team coach (5)

24 Jimmy Walker's former club (7)

Answers on page 61

Hammers Dream Team

GK – Mervyn Day
RB – Glen Johnson
CB – Rio Ferdinand
CB – Bobby Moore
LB – Frank Lampard Snr
RM – Martin Peters
CM – Trevor Brooking
CM – Michael Carrick
LM – Joe Cole
CF – Geoff Hurst
CF – Tony Cottee

West Ham United fans always enjoy listing their all-time team of favourite players – and here is just one such example.

displays at right-back. However, relegation meant sacrifices had to be made and Glen, who would earn England recognition, was off to Chelsea before ending up an FA Cup winner at Portsmouth, the club he represents to distinction today.

Rio Ferdinand

Rio is undoubtedly one of the most natural footballers ever to have graced the Academy. His debut came in May 1996 and international recognition followed 18 months later with him finishing the 1997/98 campaign as Hammer of the Year aged 20. In November 2000, he was sold for a world-record £18m fee for a defender to Leeds United but it is at Manchester United, where he headed in July 2002, that the centre-back has truly excelled. Simply one of the world's top defenders.

Mervyn Day

Now the assistant manager at West Ham United, Mervyn was the PFA Young Player of the Year in 1975. He made his debut in August 1973 as an 18-year-old and was established as first-choice goalkeeper two seasons later when the club won its second FA Cup and he was still only 19. He stayed until July 1979 before moving to Leyton Orient. Day returned as assistant manager in December 2006.

Bobby Moore

One of English football's leading lights. In his remarkable career, the legendary Barking-born defender served West Ham United with distinction between 1958 and 1974 (playing 643 times) before a three-year stint with Fulham. Moore helped the Hammers to FA Cup and European Cup Winners' Cup glory as well as winning 108 England caps and lifting the World Cup trophy in the 1966 final at Wembley. The four-time Hammer of the Year died in 1993 at the age of 51.

Glen Johnson

Glen burst on to the scene in the 2002/03 season, having had a successful loan spell at Millwall earlier in the campaign. His debut came on 22 January and 15 league and cup games later, he had established himself as a first-team regular with some commanding

Frank Lampard Sr

One of the finest defenders to ever wear the claret and blue, he was born nearby in East Ham and went on to play 664 games for the club after his debut in November 1967. A two-time FA Cup winner, he won two England caps

and will forever remain in Hammers folklore for a certain goal at Elland Road against Everton in the 1980 cup semi-final when he danced around the corner flag. The left-back also served as assistant manager alongside Harry Redknapp.

Martin Peters

A versatile midfielder who made 364 league and cup appearances for West Ham United, scoring 100 goals, he was part of the famed side that won the FA Cup and European Cup Winners' Cup and then helped England win the 1966 World Cup. Peters made it 2-1 in the final and, but for the last-gasp German equaliser in normal time, it would have been the winner. The 1964/65 Hammer of the Year went on to serve Tottenham Hotspur and Norwich City but his name was made in east London.

Trevor Brooking

Trevor was voted Hammer of the Year an unparalleled five times and this cultured midfielder's crowning moment was heading the winner in the 1980 FA Cup final, having played his part in the 1975 success. He made 637 appearances between 1967 and 1984 and scored 102 goals. Brooking was the definitive one-club man, even serving as caretaker manager twice in 2003. Capped 47 times, with five goals, Brooking was knighted in June 2004 and is still serving the Football Association as director of football development.

Michael Carrick

Although hailing from the north-east, he owes his rise to the very top of English football to his development in east London. Spotted at the famed Wallsend Boys Club in Newcastle, this elegant international midfielder headed south and linked up with Joe Cole at an early age. He played his part in the famed 1999 FA Youth Cup-winning side and would make 159 appearances up to May 2004. He moved on to Tottenham

Hotspur before joining Manchester United where he recently won the Champions League.

Joe Cole

Captain of West Ham United at just 21, this stylish midfielder remains one of the most gifted players to have emerged from the Academy. His potential was spotted at an extremely early age and it was no surprise the midfielder made his debut aged 17 in January 1999. He played 150 times for the club before relegation at the end of 2002/03 saw Chelsea swoop to take the reigning Hammer of the Year across London. He has since established himself for club and country but has never forgotten his roots.

Tony Cottee

A natural goalscorer who burst on to the scene as a 17-year-old with a New Year's Day 1983 goal against Tottenham Hotspur. He never stopped scoring after that. In all, he hit 145 goals in 335 league and cup games – a phenomenal record over two spells at the club that included 26 goals in the memorable 1985/86 season when he was Hammer of the Year and also the PFA Young Player of the Year. Cottee also earned England recognition and had success at Everton and Leicester City

Geoff Hurst

A hat-trick on 30 July 1966 may have lodged this striker's name in the history of the global game when he helped secure England's World Cup victory but there was much more before and after that historic treble. 249 goals in 500 league and cup appearances alone will testify to that. Between 1960 and 1972, the fearsome finisher was the scourge of defenders everywhere. He played his part in FA Cup and European Cup Winners' Cup success and also enjoyed a spell with Stoke City later in his career. This three-time Hammer of the Year was knighted in 1998.

10 facts about
Scott Parker

He has represented England at every level
from Under-15s to seniors.

He was born in Lambeth.

He was featured doing keepy-ups in a famous
TV advert for McDonalds
at the age of 13.

His footballing inspiration
was Paul Gascoigne.

If he hadn't been a footballer he
would have been a lorry driver.

His favourite place
in the world is Portugal.

He has a boat licence.

His favourite food is Chinese and sweet
and sour chicken in particular.

His worst habit is biting his nails.

He has three sons.

MUMBO
JUMBLE

Help! The letters in these West Ham United players' names have been all mixed up – can you put them in the right order to spell them out?

A DINNER FONDANT   _   _   _   _   _   _   _

BORN TREE REG   _   _   _   _   _

FEAR DRESS   _   _   _   _   _   _

HONDAS NEAT   _   _   _   _   _

AMONG THERE WITH TENT   _   _   _   _

THAMES UPTOWN   _   _   _   _   _

BARK MELON   _   _   _   _   _

RACCOON TELL   _   _   _   _

ARMY CONCRETE EGG   _   _   _   _   _   _

ALIEN CULLS   _   _   _   _

MILKY MEW JAR   _   _   _   _

A LYRIC GAMBLE   _   _

YORKER DINE   _   _   _   _

RACK SPOTTER   _   _   _   _   _

Answers on page 61

SUMMER SIGNINGS

Although the return to fitness and form of Julien Faubert, Scott Parker and Craig Bellamy felt like three new signings for West Ham United in summer 2008 there were plenty of fresh faces as well.

Holmar Orn Eyjolfsson

Among them was Valon Behrami, the versatile Swiss star who moved to the Boleyn Ground in a £5m deal from Lazio. He agreed a five-year contract and could not hide his delight at swapping Serie A for the Premier League.

"At Lazio, the supporters are very passionate and let you know what they think, good and bad," he said after putting pen to paper. "West Ham fans seem very passionate too I am very much looking forward to playing in front of them."

He added: "I know that there are very good players here, like Craig Bellamy and Dean Ashton and many more who I am looking forward to playing alongside." It was a former Hammers striker who helped prompt Behrami's move from Rome to London.

Former Lazio legend Paolo Di Canio spoke fondly of his time in claret and blue, as Behrami recalled. "I talked to Paolo many times. He talked a lot about West Ham but also about football in this country and in particular the Premier League. So that is why it is a dream come true for me and I am very happy to be here."

Another who is thrilled to be with the club is highly-rated Iceland Under-21 defender Holmar Orn Eyjolfsson who joined just before Behrami in July

on a long-term contract from HK Kopavogur. Both players had been coveted throughout Europe.

The 17-year-old first spent a week on trial at Chadwell Heath the previous February, having caught the eye as he rapidly rose through the Icelandic youth ranks.

"I am really happy to sign for West Ham. I have heard of many good players that have come from the club's academy. When I was on trial in February I really enjoyed the tempo and style of training and it helped me take my talent to the next level.

"It is obviously very scary to move away from my family but it is my dream to play in England and what I have always wanted to do so that outweighs any apprehension I had about moving here."

At the end of July, the club also signed the 26-year-old Czech goalkeeper Jan Lastuvka on a one-year loan from Ukrainian club Shakhtar Donetsk.

The experienced performer joined two compatriots - the highly-rated 18-year-old, and fellow shot-stopper Marek Stech, and goalkeeping coach Ludek Miklosko, at the Boleyn Ground. A former Under-21 international, Lastuvka spent four years at Miklosko's former club Banik Ostrava, including winning the Czech title in the 2003/04 season, before moving to Ukrainian football.

Jan Lastuvka

10 facts about
Mark Noble

He was born and raised in Canning Town and grew up supporting West Ham United.

He joined the club as a schoolboy and became the youngest player ever to appear in the reserve team, aged 15.

His nickname is 'Nobes'.

He always has to be third in the lineup for luck.

The best footballer he says he's played against is Paul Scholes.

His worst habit is leaving the water in the bath after he's got out.

His footballing inspiration is Joe Cole.

He would be working as a mechanic if he hadn't been a footballer.

His favourite film is Ace Ventura, Pet Detective.

He scored on his Premier League debut against Tottenham Hotspur.

Quiz

- Which Argentine forward was voted Hammer of the Year in 2007?
- What nationality is Luis Boa Morte?
- Which two West Ham United players played together at Cardiff City?
- What is Alan Curbishley's real name?
- Who did West Ham United meet the last time they were in the FA Cup final?
- Who was the West Ham United captain before Lucas Neill?
- Which city does George McCartney hail from?
- How many players in the current squad have played for Norwich City?
- Can you name them?
- What position did assistant manager Mervyn Day play in for West Ham United?
- What colour is the club's new away kit?
- When was the last time the club won the FA Cup?
- Which team did West Ham United beat 5-0 in the 2007/08 season?
- Which former player's brother and cousin also played for West Ham United?
- Can you name them?

Wordsearch

Ashton ☐
Bellamy ☐
Blue ☐
Boleyn ☐
Bowyer ☐
Bubbles ☐
Claret ☐
Collison ☐
Curbishley ☐
Dyer ☐
Green ☐
Hammers ☐
Irons ☐
Moore ☐
Neill ☐
Noble ☐
Parker ☐
Sears ☐
Tomkins ☐
Upson ☐

```
G B C U R B I S H L E Y N B
T R L L L I E N T E R A L C
R F T O M K I N S R V L X K
N E Q X T B N N E M C B X B
O L Y L X O E V O L M X U P
T C M D X W E O C C B B V S
H O J N K Y R H Y B B O R R
S L Z M Z E G M B L U E N E
A L B P B R A I E C M H Q K
P I P O X L S S R M D J X R
Z S Y N L R Y K A O R Q M A
L O R E A E N H B C N Y K P
B N B E K P Y G M G F S R V
Y F S U P S O N N M Z L L P
```

Answers on page 61

Training Day

On Thursday 3 July, the West Ham United squad returned to Chadwell Heath to be put through their paces on the first day back in training after the summer break. Here are some exclusive pictures of the day...

10 facts about
George McCartney

He started every game for West Ham United in the 2007/08 season.

He played for Sunderland for eight years before joining West Ham United in August 2006.

His footballing inspiration is George Best.

His motto in life is to always work hard.

He is scared of flying.

His favourite place in the world is Hawaii.

His worst habit is asking people to repeat themselves.

He likes eating crisps.

The best footballer he says he's played against is Teddy Sheringham on his debut for Sunderland against Tottenham Hotspur.

He signed a new five-year deal with the club in the summer of 2008.

Did you know?

Jimmy Collins, who played for the club from 1924-36, was the first-ever West Ham United player to own a car.

Hammers fans first started singing 'Bubbles' to a player called Billy Murray in the late 1920s. Billy had curly hair and resembled a character in a painting called Bubbles, which was used in a popular advert for Pears Soap at the time.

The West Ham United players used to be given lunch vouchers in the late 1960s and chose to spend them at Cassetaris Café on the Barking Road, which still exists today. The team would meet there and discuss tactics, formations and training sessions.

West Ham United legend Len Goulden worked on the construction of Highbury stadium, laying concrete for the terraces, during the close season in the early 1930s.

Hollywood actor Ray Winstone is a lifelong Hammers fan – and actress Keira Knightley has also reportedly said that she supports West Ham United too!

The club began as Thames Ironworks FC but re-launched as West Ham United in 1900.

The team used to wear dark blue kits until, it's believed, the Hammers player Bill Dove won a race against four Aston Villa players and got to keep their claret and blue kits as a prize.

The castles on the outside of the Boleyn Ground represent a local building, Green Street House, which was known as the "Boleyn Castle" through an association with Anne Boleyn. The manor was rumoured to be one of the sites at which King Henry VIII courted his second queen.

West Ham United played in the first FA Cup final at Wembley and the last one at the Millennium Stadium, Cardiff.

Club legend Bobby Moore lifted a trophy at Wembley three years running in 1964 (FA Cup), 1965 (European Cup Winners' Cup) and 1966 (World Cup).